the pocket book of
COCKTAILS

the pocket book of
COCKTAILS

OVER 150 CLASSIC & CONTEMPORARY RECIPES

RYLAND PETERS & SMALL
LONDON • NEW YORK

Designer Paul Stradling
Editor Alice Sambrook
Production Controller Mai-Ling Collyer
Art Director Leslie Harrington
Editorial Director Julia Charles
Publisher Cindy Richards

Indexer Vanessa Bird

First published in 2016 by
Ryland Peters & Small
20–21 Jockey's Fields
London WC1R 4BW
and
341 E 116th St
New York NY 10029

www.rylandpeters.com

Text © Ben Reed, Carol Hilker, Elsa Petersen-Schepelern,
Janet Sawyer, Shelagh Ryan, Ursula Ferrigno, Valerie
Aikman-Smith, William Yeoward and Ryland Peters &
Small 2016.

Design and photographs © Ryland Peters & Small 2016

ISBN: 978-1-84975-723-2

10 9 8 7 6 5

A CIP record for this book is available from the British Library.

US Library of Congress Cataloging-in-Publication data has
been applied for.

Printed and bound in China

NOTES

- Recipes make enough to serve 1 unless stated in
  the individual introduction.

- Measurements are occasionally given in barspoons,
  which are equivalent to 5 ml or 1 teaspoon.

- Ice cubes or crushed ice are not stated in
  ingredients but are useful for most recipes.

- All fruit and vegetables should be washed
  thoroughly before consumption. Unwaxed citrus
  fruits should be used whenever possible.

- All eggs are large (US) or medium (UK), unless
  specified as US extra-large, in which case UK large
  should be used. Uncooked or partially cooked eggs
  should not be served to the very old, frail, young
  children, pregnant women or those with
  compromised immune systems.

- Both British (Metric) and American (Imperial plus
  US cups) are included in these recipes for your
  convenience – however it is important to work with
  one set of measurements and not alternate
  between the two within a recipe.

CONTENTS

INTRODUCTION

The Pocket Book of Cocktails brings you over 150 recipes to choose from; never again will you find yourself without the perfect drink in hand. Whether hosting a sophisticated soirée, a tiki beach party, planning a festive get-together, or simply indulging alone – a cocktail is one of the finest treats in life.

With this go-to guide for the aspiring mixologist, learn about essential tools, equipment and glassware, and become a fountain of cocktail knowledge for your friends and family by taking note of the neat little introduction to each drink.

Choose from the flirty sophistication of the **vodka** chapter with a classic Cosmopolitan or Vodka Espresso. Try a grown-up classic from the **gin** section such as the Negroni or Singapore Sling. Transport yourself to a sun-drenched beach bar with a **rum**-based Piña Colada or Raspberry and Rose Mojito. Indulge in the old-fashioned wholesomeness of a **whiskey** Mint Julep or Salted Caramel Bourbon Milkshake. Find fun and summery drinks like the Frozen Peach Margarita or Salty Chihuahua in the **tequila** section. Old favourites such as a Sidecar or Brandy Alexander are brought to the forefront in **brandy, liqueurs and aperitifs**. And for something really special flip to the **champagne and wine** section for a Limoncello Champagne or Al Fresco Bellini recipe.

Here you'll find a range of tasty beverages from revived vintage classics to modern and trendy creations. Get shaking, stirring and making – join the cocktail revolution!

EQUIPMENT

For the aspiring bartender, getting the right equipment can be as important as the taste of the final drink itself. You will probably find that you already have most of what you need to make cocktails in your own kitchen. But if you want to create the right atmosphere for your guests and mix cocktails with a little more flair, it's worth getting a few accessories.

Measure/Jigger

Measures/jiggers come in a variety of sizes so you can pour the correct quantity of drink. The dual measure is a good choice, where one end holds 25 ml and the other holds 50 ml in the UK, or 1 oz. and 2 oz. in the US.

Shaker

Shake it up, baby! There are two basic types of shaker: the three-piece (or deco) shaker and the Boston shaker. They come in all shapes and sizes, from fire extinguishers to rockets.

Mixing Glass

This is used for making drinks that are stirred, not shaken.

Barspoon

Handy for both stirring drinks and for the gentle pouring required for layering drinks. The flat end can be used for muddling or crushing ingredients. The barspoon holds around the same amount of liquid as a regular teaspoon.

Muddler

A long pestle that's used for mixing or crushing ingredients such as sugar cubes, lemons or limes.

Strainer

There are two types of strainer: the Hawthorn strainer that will sit over the metal part of the shaker, and the Julep that fits comfortably in the mixing glass.

Straws
A simple straw is a hygienic way to test the taste of your tipple. Dip it into the drink and place your finger over the top end to create a vacuum. Take the straw out and suck the liquid to see if it needs anything to be added.

Blender
To whizz up your drinks.

Juicer
Useful when extracting the juice from fruits.

Swizzle Sticks
Used for stirring drinks. Plus it's fun to say.

Quality Paring Knife and Peeler
A paring knife has a small sharp blade that makes it easier to complete fiddly or intricate jobs. A sharp peeler will make it much easier to prepare attractive garnishes.

GLASSWARE

When choosing the glass in which to serve your drink, first choose the appropriate size, a highball for a long mixed drink, or an old-fashioned rocks glass for a short drink. The glassware used for a specific drink is designed to suit its composition: the champagne glass is tall and thin to maintain the bubbles, the whiskey tumbler is squat to allow the drink's aroma to swirl around the glass. The following list of glasses should be all you need to show off your taste sensations. Remember, presentation is key!

Shot Glass (1)
Pretty self-explanatory, this small glass holds either a single or a double shot of liquor. Shooters (mixed layered shots such as the B52 p.149) are also served in these glasses.

Tumbler (2)
Also known as an old-fashioned glass, rocks glass or lowball glass, a tumbler is used for short drinks over ice.

Highball Glass (3)
This is a tall, thin glass used for serving long cocktails and summery drinks. Plenty of room for mixing fresh fruit and ice.

Heatproof Glass (4)
A handled glass means you won't burn your fingers when slurping a hot toddy, mulled wine or Irish coffee. They are generally made of heat-resistant material that won't crack if filled with very hot liquid.

Champagne Flute (5)
A tall, narrow glass that houses the bubbly stuff. Cheers!

Wine Glass (6)
A glass that, er, holds wine. Some say the shape of a well-made wine glass can influence the flavour, so choose carefully.

Martini Glass (7)

A must for any aspiring mixologist, this glass has a cone-shaped bowl atop a stem. Cocktails served in a martini glass should be chilled, and the long stem allows the drinker to hold it without affecting the temperature.

Margarita Coupette (8)

Similar to a martini glass but larger and curved. Lovely for fruity or tropical cocktails.

Hurricane Glass (9)

Hold onto your hats! Also known as a tulip glass, this generally holds punches and frozen drinks. It's similarly shaped to a vase and is typically taller and wider than a highball glass.

Jug/Pitcher (not pictured)

A large container, usually with a handle and spout for pouring. Holds many servings so perfect for drinks like punch or sangria.

VODKA

CLASSIC MARTINI
pictured opposite

15 ml/½ oz. dry vermouth
75 ml/3 oz. vodka
twist of lemon zest
2 unstuffed green olives,
to garnish

Perhaps the most iconic of all aperitifs, this elegant drink is perfect for any classy occasion. James Bond eat your heart out.

- Pour the vermouth and vodka over ice in a mixing jug/pitcher. Stir to make the cocktail very cold. Strain into a martini glass. Hold the lemon zest over the glass and twist to spray a fine mist of its oils onto the cocktail. Discard the zest and garnish the martini with olives speared on a toothpick.

BREAKFAST MARTINI

Not recommended to accompany your cornflakes, unless early morning is actually last thing at night for you.

50 ml/2 oz. vodka
2 barspoons marmalade

- Pour a large shot of vodka into a shaker filled with ice, add the marmalade, shake sharply and strain into a frosted martini glass.

APPLE MARTINI *pictured opposite*

20 ml/⅔ oz. apple schnapps
40 ml/1½ oz. vanilla vodka
25 ml/1 oz. apple juice
2 barspoons fresh lime juice
2 barspoons sugar syrup (page 91)
very thin slices of green- and pink-skinned apple; ½ a vanilla pod/bean, to garnish

Vanilla and apple work beautifully together in this delicious martini. Use the kooky sliced apple garnish pictured to jazz up the slightly plain colour.

- Put all the ingredients into a cocktail shaker filled with ice. Shake. Strain into a martini glass. Garnish with the apple and vanilla. (If the apple slices are freshly cut, they will 'stick' together in a row.)

RASPBERRY MARTINI

This lovely pink drink should be quite thick in consistency, it should flow down your throat like treacle.

- Shake all the ingredients in a shaker filled with ice and strain into a pre-chilled martini glass. Garnish with two raspberries.

50 ml/2 oz. vodka
a dash of framboise
a dash of orange bitters
15 ml/½ oz. raspberry purée
2 fresh raspberries, to garnish

FRENCH MARTINI *pictured opposite*

50 ml/2 oz. vodka

a large dash of Chambord
(or crème de mure)

75 ml/3 oz. pineapple juice

The French Martini is great for parties and simple to make in bulk. Shake hard when preparing and you will be rewarded with a thick white froth on the surface.

• Add all the ingredients to a shaker filled with ice, shake sharply and strain into a frosted martini glass.

TURKISH CHOCOLATE MARTINI

This drink is pure indulgence. The heaviness of the crème de cacao combines with the lightness of the flower water to create a truly Turkish delight.

• Add all the ingredients to a shaker filled with ice, shake well, then strain into a chilled martini glass edged with cocoa powder.

50 ml/2 oz. vodka

2 barspoons white crème de cacao

2 dashes of rose water

cocoa powder, for the glass

POLISH MARTINI *pictured opposite*

25 ml/1 oz. Krupnik vodka
25 ml/1 oz. Zubrowka vodka
25 ml/1 oz. apple juice

The bitterness of Zubrowka with the potent sweetness of Krupnik combine with the crispness of apple juice to create a beguiling depth of taste.

- Pour the two vodkas and the apple juice into a mixing glass filled with ice. Stir and strain into a chilled martini glass.

GOTHAM MARTINI

A cocktail that is as sinister and mysterious as the name suggests. Try varying the amount of black Sambuca for a darker, more thrilling result.

60 ml/2¼ oz. frozen Stolichnaya vodka
a dash of black Sambuca

- Pour the vodka into a chilled martini glass, gently add the Sambuca, then serve.

COSMOPOLITAN *pictured opposite*

35 ml/1¼ oz. lemon vodka
20 ml/⅔ oz. triple sec
20 ml/⅔ oz. fresh lime juice
25 ml/1 oz. cranberry juice
lemon zest, to garnish

'Hi, I'd like a cheeseburger, please, large fries and a Cosmopolitan' – Carrie Bradshaw. This sassy cocktail is just as good with fancy nibbles as with fast food.

- Add all the ingredients to a shaker filled with ice, shake sharply and strain into a chilled martini glass. Garnish with lemon zest for that extra zing!

COSMO ROYALE

For a fizzy spin, add a float of champagne The bubbles will happily sit on the surface if you pour them gently!

- Add all the ingredients, except the champagne, to a shaker filled with ice. Shake sharply and strain into a chilled martini glass. Float the champagne on the surface and garnish with orange zest.

35 ml/1¼ oz. lemon vodka
15 ml/½ oz. fresh lime juice
15 ml/½ oz. Cointreau
25 ml/1 oz. cranberry juice
champagne, to float
orange zest, to garnish

METROPOLITAN

pictured opposite

35 ml/1¼ oz. Absolut Kurant vodka or other blackcurrant flavoured spirit

20 ml/⅔ oz. triple sec

20 ml/⅔ oz. fresh lime juice

25 ml/1 oz. cranberry juice

orange zest, to garnish

This cocktail is a fruity variation on the Cosmopolitan. Blackcurrant vodka, combined with cranberry and lime juices.

- Shake all the ingredients sharply over ice and strain into a chilled martini glass.

- To make a flaming orange zest, squeeze the oil from a strip of orange zest, held skin downwards and over a flame above the glass. Rub the rim with the orange zest before dropping it into the glass.

METROPOLIS

The Metropolis features an addition of champagne and berry-flavoured liqueur, inspired by the much-loved Kir Royale.

- Shake the vodka and the crème de framboise together over ice and strain into a martini glass. Top with champagne and serve.

25 ml/1 oz. vodka

25 ml/1 oz. crème de framboise

champagne, to top up

HARVEY WALLBANGER

50 ml/2 oz. vodka
15 ml/½ oz. Galliano
orange juice, to top up
orange slice, to garnish

The story goes that Harvey, a Californian surfer who had performed particularly badly in an important contest, visited his local bar to drown his sorrows. He ordered his usual Screwdriver — only to decide that it wasn't strong enough for what he had in mind. Scanning the bar for something to boost his drink, his eyes fell on the distinctively shaped Galliano bottle, a shot of which was then added to his drink as a float.

- Build the ingredients over ice into a highball glass, stir and serve with an orange slice.

SEA BREEZE

The Sea Breeze is a modern, thirst-quenching variation on the classic Screwdriver. The cranberry juice lends a light, fruity, refreshing quality and combines with the bitter grapefruit juice, making it very popular with people who don't particularly enjoy the taste of alcohol.

50 ml/2 oz. vodka
150 ml/⅔ cup cranberry juice
50 ml/2 oz. grapefruit juice
lime wedge, to garnish

- Pour the vodka into a highball glass filled with ice. Three-quarters fill the glass with cranberry juice and top with fresh grapefruit juice. Garnish with a lime wedge and serve with a straw.

BERRY CAIPIROSKA

pictured opposite

50 ml/2 oz. vodka

4 lime wedges

2 white sugar cubes

3 fresh berries, plus extra
to garnish

(strawberries, raspberries or
blueberries)

When it's hot outside this delicious summery cocktail is perfectly refreshing. It can be made to taste with fresh berries of your choosing.

• Muddle all the ingredients in a rock glass with a wooden pestle. Top up with crushed ice and stir gently to mix. Serve garnished with a few fresh berries skewered onto a toothpick.

QUEEN OF TARTS

(pictured page 100, left)

With its cheeky name and adventurous flavour, this balsamic strawberry temptress is perfect for serving at parties.

• Combine all of the ingredients and serve over ice in a martini glass.

75 ml/3 oz. dry martini

50 ml/2 oz. vodka

freshly squeezed juice of ½ lemon

3 teaspoons caster/granulated sugar

3 barspoons balsamic vinegar

6 strawberries, puréed

LEGEND

50 ml/2 oz. vodka
25 ml/1 oz. crème de mure
25 ml/1 oz. fresh lime juice
a dash sugar syrup (page 91)
lemon zest, to garnish
(optional)

Invented in London in the late 1980s by Dick Bradsell, this recipe has to be followed closely, as too much of any of the ingredients can result in an unpalatable cocktail. Make sure you taste each concoction before you serve it.

• Add all the ingredients to a shaker filled with ice, shake sharply and strain into a chilled martini glass. Garnish with lemon zest.

Mix It Up

Try replacing the crème de mure with your berry liqueur of choice: a scrumptious crème de fraise, crème de framboise or crème de cassis.

SILVER STREAK

25 ml/1 oz. chilled vodka
25 ml/1 oz. kummel

Kummel is one of the least frequently used liqueurs in cocktails, more's the pity. It has a distinctive, almost aniseed–like taste that comes from the caraway seeds used in its production, and as an added bonus it promotes good digestion. For best results keep both the vodka and the kummel in a fridge or freezer and pour them gently into a sturdy old–fashioned glass for the perfect after–dinner nightcap.

• Pour a generous single measure of chilled vodka into a rocks glass filled with ice. Add a similar amount of kummel, stir gently and serve.

Mix It Up

To inject some zesty zing into this simple drink, add 25 ml/ 1 oz. fresh lime juice and plenty of ice to the rest of the ingredients in a cocktail shaker. Shake well and strain into a chilled glass.

BLACK RUSSIAN
pictured opposite, left

50 ml/2 oz. vodka
25 ml/1 oz. Kahlúa
stemmed cherry, to garnish

The Black and White Russians are classics that have been on the scene for many years. They make stylish after-dinner cocktails with their sweet coffee flavour, which is sharpened up by the vodka.

• Shake the vodka and Kahlúa together over ice. Strain into a rocks glass filled with ice. Garnish with a stemmed cherry.

WHITE RUSSIAN
pictured opposite, right

The White Russian, with its addition of the cream float, is great served as a nightcap.

• To make a White Russian, make a Black Russian (see above) then layer a tablespoon of single cream into the glass over the back of a barspoon. As before, garnish with a stemmed cherry.

50 ml/2 oz. vodka
25 ml/1 oz. Kahlúa
25 ml/¾ oz. single/light cream
stemmed cherry, to garnish

VODKA ESPRESSO

50 ml/2 oz. fresh espresso coffee

50 ml/2 oz. vodka

a dash of sugar syrup (page 91)

3 coffee beans, to garnish

The dark and delicious Vodka Espresso is designed to awaken its recipient.

- Pour the espresso coffee into a shaker, add the vodka and sugar syrup to taste, shake the mixture sharply and strain into an old-fashioned glass filled with ice. Garnish with three coffee beans.

ALMOND VODKA ESPRESSO

pictured opposite

A less than innocent concoction, composed of amaretto and vodka as well as a coffee liqueur. The amount of sugar you include in the espresso is up to you.

- Pour all the ingredients into a shaker. Fill with ice and shake. Strain into a martini glass. Wait for the cocktail to 'separate'– a foam will rise to the top and the liquid below become clearer. Garnish with the coffee beans and almonds.

25 ml/1 oz. freshly made espresso, sweetened to taste

35 ml/1¼ oz. vodka

20 ml/⅔ oz. amaretto

15 ml/½ oz. Kahlúa or other Coffee liqueur

3 coffee beans and a pinch of toasted, flaked/slivered almonds, to garnish

BEST EVER BLOODY MARY

500 ml/2 cups tomato juice

400 g/2½ cups cherry tomatoes

30 ml/2 tablespoons Worcestershire sauce

30 ml/2 tablespoons Sriracha Chilli sauce

a 3-cm/1¼-inch piece of horseradish, finely grated

sea salt and freshly ground black pepper

60 ml/¼ cup fresh lime juice

300 ml/1¼ cups vodka

celery, to garnish

chilli/dried hot pepper flakes, to garnish

A Bloody Mary is the ultimate brunch drink, allowing you to ingest booze before midday with complete legitimacy. This recipe makes enough to serve 4 – a hangover shared is a hangover solved.

- Put the tomato juice and cherry tomatoes in a food processor and blend until smooth.

- Transfer to a jug/pitcher and stir in the Worcestershire sauce, Sriracha chilli sauce and grated horseradish. Season with salt and pepper, cover with clingfilm/plastic wrap and chill in the fridge for at least 30 minutes.

- When ready to serve, add the lime juice and vodka, and stir well. Place a pickled celery stick in 4 high-ball glasses, fill each glass with ice and pour in the Bloody Mary mixture. Garnish each with a pinch of chilli/dried red pepper flakes and enjoy!

Mix It Up

For extra depth of flavour try roasting the cherry tomatoes before blending.

GIN

CLASSIC GIN MARTINI
pictured opposite

a dash of vermouth

75 ml/3 oz. well-chilled gin

an olive or lemon twist,
to garnish

Stirring a martini to make the perfect mix is the original labour of love for any bartender. Add less vermouth for a 'dry' martini and more vermouth for a 'wet'.

- Add both the ingredients to a mixing glass filled with ice and stir. Strain into a chilled martini glass and garnish with an olive or lemon twist.

SMOKY MARTINI

Adding a dash of smoky whiskey in place of vermouth makes the martini an altogether different beast.

50 ml/2 oz. gin

a dash of dry vermouth

a dash of whisky

an olive, to garnish

- Add the ingredients to a shaker filled with cracked ice. Shake sharply and strain into a frosted martini glass with a lemon-zested rim. Garnish with an olive.

TOKYO MARTINI *pictured opposite*

50 ml/2 oz. gin
2 thin strips of fresh ginger
a small roll of wasabi
ginger strip, to garnish

This martini can be a bit intense if it is made without care. Try to find the best–quality wasabi and the freshest ginger.

• Add the ingredients to a shaker filled with ice, shake and strain into a frosted martini glass. Garnish with a thin strip of ginger.

SAPPHIRE MARTINI

A drizzle of Parfait Amour, a beautiful orange curaçao flavoured with violets, combined with chilled Bombay Sapphire gin produces a magnificent cocktail.

2 barspoons Parfait Amour
50 ml/2 oz. chilled Bombay Sapphire gin
fresh blueberries, to garnish

• Gently pour the Parfait Amour into a chilled martini glass. Pour the gin (which should have been in the freezer for at least 1 hour) over a barspoon, so that it sits over the liqueur. Garnish with blueberries on a toothpick.

TOM COLLINS

50 ml/2 oz. gin

20 ml/⅔ oz. fresh lemon juice

15 ml/½ oz fresh fruit purée (pomegranate, raspberry, and blueberry purées are all good)

sugar syrup, to taste (page 91)

soda water, to top up

seasonal fresh fruit, to garnish

Although many consider the Tom Collins to be an English drink, this early punch was actually first documented by Professor Jerry Thomas, the father of American cocktails, in 1876. It has remained a cocktail-party classic ever since.

• Add all the ingredients except the soda water to a highball glass filled with ice and stir gently to mix. Top up with soda water and stir again. Garnish with seasonal fresh fruit.

Mix It Up

The Tom Collins is a close relation of the Elderflower Collins. To make one of these, replace the fresh fruit purée with 15 ml/½ oz. elderflower cordial. Garnish with a slice of lemon and a sprig of fresh mint leaves. The botanicals in the gin get an unexpected boost from the elderflower, making this a delicate cocktail full of floral flavours.

SLOE GIN FIZZ

50 ml/2 oz. sloe gin

20 ml/⅔ oz. fresh lemon juice

a dash of sugar syrup
(page 91)

soda water, to top up

lemon slice, to garnish

You may need to play around with the balance of flavours in this cocktail, as different brands of sloe gin have varying degrees of sweetness.

- Add all the ingredients, except the soda, to a shaker filled with ice. Shake sharply and strain into a highball glass filled with ice.

- Top with soda water, garnish with a lemon slice and serve with two straws.

RAMOS GIN FIZZ

Created by Henry Ramos, a saloon owner from New Orleans. Henry maintained that his Gin Fizz should be shaken for at least 5 minutes to achieve the right consistency. He even hired additional bartenders for this very purpose.

50 ml/2 oz. gin
25 ml/1 oz. single/light cream
20 ml/⅔ oz. egg white
20 ml/⅔ oz. fresh lemon juice
20 ml/⅔ oz. fresh lime juice
20 ml/⅔ oz. sugar syrup (page 91)
2 dashes of orange-flower water
a dash of soda water

- Add all the ingredients, except the soda, to a shaker filled with ice. Shake sharply for as long as you can, then shake some more.

- Strain the fluffy mixture into a chilled champagne flute, add a dash of soda water and serve.

NEGRONI

25 ml/1 oz. Martini Rosso
vermouth

25 ml/1 oz. gin

25 ml/1 oz. Campari

orange wedges, to garnish

This is surely the Italian cocktail par excellence. Its flavour is a splendid fusion of sweetness, spiciness and bitterness, giving it a particular kind of 'strength' that might be considered to be a reflection of Italian character. It is also deep and rich in colour, an attractive drink all round.

- Fill an old-fashioned glass with ice. Pour in the ingredients and gently stir. Garnish with the orange wedges.

Mix It Up

If you prefer a taste that is less bitter, try a White Negroni. Make this by replacing the vermouth with Lillet Blanc and replacing the Campari with Suze. Garnish with grapefruit or orange zest.

MARTINEZ

50 ml/2 oz. Old Tom gin
15 ml/½ oz. sweet vermouth
a dash of orange bitters
a dash of maraschino liqueur
lemon twist, to garnish

The Martinez is believed to be the first documented martini, dating back as far as 1849. Its sweet flavours were geared to appeal to the taste buds of the time and the availability of certain spirits. This is a variation on a recipe from Jerry Thomas.

• Add all the ingredients to a shaker filled with ice, shake and strain into a chilled martini glass. Garnish with a lemon twist.

Mix It Up

If you don't have maraschino, kirsch can be used instead. This will produce a drink that is less sweet. If you still want it sweet, add a dash of sugar syrup (page 91).

GIN BRAMBLE *pictured opposite*

50 ml/2 oz. gin

25 ml/1 oz. fresh lemon juice

2 barspoons sugar syrup (page 91)

15 ml/½ oz. crème de mure

a lemon wedge and a blackberry, to garnish

This is a perfect cocktail for drinking on a sunny deck in the cool of an early evening — blissful!

• Build the gin, lemon juice and sugar syrup over crushed ice in a rocks glass and stir. Drizzle the crème de mure over the ice and garnish with a lemon wedge and a fresh blackberry.

GIN GIMLET

Be sparing with the lime cordial, the Gimlet is among those drinks that can be ruined if the gin is drowned out.

50 ml/2 oz. gin

25 ml/1 oz. lime cordial

• Pour the gin and cordial into a shaker filled with ice. Shake very sharply and strain into a frosted martini glass.

CLOVER CLUB

50 ml/2 oz. gin

20 ml/⅔ oz. fresh lemon juice

2 barspoons raspberry syrup

a dash of egg white

sugar syrup, to taste
(page 91)

Invented around the turn of the last century, this drink was named after a group of high-fliers that would meet at the Bellevue-Stratford Hotel in Philadelphia. Try to use some raspberry syrup or make your own with fresh raspberries and sugar.

- Add all the ingredients to a shaker filled with ice and shake sharply. Strain into a chilled cocktail glass.

Mix It Up

A Royal Clover Club is a variation of the Clover Club that contains an egg yolk instead of egg white. This will slightly alter the texture and the colour to a rich orangey pink. Always make sure to use the best quality organic eggs in cocktails such as these.

GARRICK GIN PUNCH

50 ml/2 oz. London dry gin

25 ml/1 oz. fresh lemon juice

15 ml/½ oz. maraschino liqueur

a dash of sugar syrup (page 91)

2 dashes of Angostura bitters

lemon zest, to garnish

If the dryness of a good London gin is your thing then this is your cocktail. A superb aperitif, this cocktail will cut through the fug of your day and prepare your palate for whatever the evening holds. Shake it until it's as cold as can be and serve in a chilled glass.

- Add all the ingredients to a cocktail shaker filled with ice and shake together until the outside of the shaker starts to frost.

- Strain into a frosted coupette glass and serve garnished with a thin piece of lemon zest.

Mix It Up

Fresh lime juice works well in place of the lemon juice and adds a pleasing green tinge to the drink.

SINGAPORE SLING

25 ml/1 oz. gin

25 ml/1 oz. cherry brandy

1 barspoon Benedictine

25 ml/1 oz. fresh lemon juice

a small dash of Angostura bitters

soda water, to top up

lemon zest curls and cocktail cherries, to garnish

Created at the Long Bar at the Raffles hotel in Singapore, when this drink is made correctly, and without using one of the cheap pre-mixes that are so prevalent today, it is the peak of sophistication! The original recipe has long been a subject of hot debate; this is one of the best.

- Put all the ingredients in a small pitcher/jug filled with ice and stir gently to mix. Top up with soda water.

- Serve in a tall, ice-filled glass, garnished with a lemon zest curl and a cocktail cherry.

Mix It Up

If this cocktail tickles your fancy then you could also try the Chinatown Sling. Simply replace the lemon juice with pineapple juice and garnish with cocktail cherries and a pineapple triangle.

WATERMELON GIN

½ very ripe watermelon, well chilled

50 ml/2 oz. gin (or to taste)

sprigs of fresh mint and watermelon triangles, to garnish

The summery flavour of ripe red watermelon goes wonderfully well with the fresh, clean, lemony taste of gin. The seed-free section in the middle of a melon is the sweetest, so if you're cutting pieces for a garnish use this part.

- Cut the watermelon in half and remove the rind and seeds. Whizz the flesh in a food processor. If the mixture is too thick, add water.

- Pour into a jug/pitcher, stir in the gin and serve in small glasses with plenty of crushed ice, a sprig of mint and a melon triangle.

Mix It Up

Cantaloupe melon can be used in place of watermelon – due to its firmer texture whizz for slightly longer in the food processor. Lovely with a dash of elderflower liqueur.

WHITE LADY WITH VANILLA

50 ml/2 oz. gin
15 ml/½ oz. fresh lemon juice
15 ml/½ oz. Cointreau
½ a vanilla pod/bean

Vanilla is a modern addition to the classic version of a White Lady, it helps to round out and deepen the flavour. A classy and delicious cocktail, perfect for any ladies who lunch, or men for that matter.

- Place the gin, lemon juice, Cointreau and vanilla pod/bean (split if you'd like the seeds to add extra vanilla flavour to your cocktail) in a cocktail shaker with a few ice cubes.

- Shake very well with ice, remove the vanilla pod/bean, and serve in a cocktail glass.

Mix It Up

To enhance your cocktail why not split a vanilla pod/bean and put it in a jar of sugar for two weeks or more, then use the sugar on the rim of your cocktail glass. Wet the rim of your glass with lemon juice and then dip into the sugar.

WHISKEY

MINT JULEP

15 ml/½ oz. sugar syrup
(page 91)
3 fresh mint sprigs
60 ml/2¼ oz. bourbon

First consumed in the late 1700s, the granddaddy of cocktails was traditionally served on Kentucky Derby Day. These days it's a cocktail for the more discerning amongst us.

- Muddle the sugar syrup, one mint sprig and the bourbon in a rocks glass. Add crushed ice and garnish with the remaining mint sprigs. Serve with two straws.

Mix It Up
For a different take on this classic, use brandy instead of bourbon to create a Brandy Mint Julep.

PERFECT MANHATTAN *pictured opposite*

50 ml/2 oz. rye whiskey
15 ml/½ oz. sweet vermouth
15 ml/½ oz. dry vermouth
a dash of Angostura bitters
orange zest, to garnish

'Perfect' does not refer to how well the drink is put together, it describes the perfect balance between sweet and dry.

- Add the ingredients to a mixing glass filled with ice (first ensure all the ingredients are very cold) and stir the mixture until chilled. Strain into a frosted martini glass, add the garnish and serve.

SWEET MANHATTAN

For those with a sweet tooth, the addition of orange bitters provides a subtle shift in flavour to this classic drink.

- Add the ingredients to a mixing glass filled with ice (first ensure all the ingredients are very cold) and stir the mixture until chilled. Strain into a frosted martini glass, add the garnish and serve.

50 ml/2 oz. rye whiskey
25 ml/1 oz. sweet vermouth
a dash of orange bitters
maraschino cherry, to garnish

ROB ROY

pictured opposite

50 ml/2 oz. Scotch whisky
20 ml/⅔ oz. sweet vermouth
a dash of Angostura bitters
lemon zest, to garnish

Have fun choosing from the vast range of whiskies available to star in this cocktail.

- Add all the ingredients to a mixing glass filled with ice and stir gently with a barspoon. Strain into a chilled rocks glass filled with ice and garnish with a thin piece of lemon zest.

CARAMEL ROB ROY

Judging by the name of this cocktail, there can't be much doubt that we shall be having a 'wee dram'. What a treat this becomes with the caramel syrup.

- Pour all the ingredients into a shaker or mixing jug. Add ice and stir vigorously. Double-strain into a coupe glass. Mist with the orange twist. Run the twist around the rim of the glass, then drop it gently into the cocktail.

2 barspoons Antica Formula vermouth

2 barspoons Noilly Prat dry vermouth

2 barspoons caramel syrup

50 ml/2 oz. Bowmore 12-year-old malt whisky

6 drops of orange bitters

orange twist, to garnish

OLD-FASHIONED *pictured opposite*

1 sugar cube

2 dashes of Angostura bitters

50 ml/2 oz. rye whiskey or bourbon

orange zest, to garnish

During the prohibition era, strong flavourings such as Angostura bitters were used in cocktails to disguise the taste of illegally-produced spirits, or 'moonshine'.

- Muddle all the ingredients in a rocks glass, adding ice as you go. Garnish with orange zest and serve.

WALNUT & MAPLE OLD-FASHIONED

This is a cocktail that comes into its own in the fall/autumn, when the inclusion of nuts is especially fitting.

- Muddle the orange in an old-fashioned glass. Add the rest of the ingredients and fill with ice cubes. Stir slowly for a minute or so to allow the ice to dilute the bourbon slightly and for the flavours to develop. Garnish with the orange zest.

2 half-slices orange

2 barspoons maple syrup

2 barspoons walnut syrup

6 drops of orange bitters

60 ml/2 oz. walnut-infused bourbon whiskey

orange zest, to garnish

WHISKEY SAZERAC

50 ml/2 oz. rye whiskey

2 barspoons sugar syrup (page 91)

2 dashes of Peychaud's bitters

2 barspoons absinthe, to rinse the glass

thin lemon zest, to garnish

One of the earliest recorded cocktails, the Sazerac probably came into this world in the 1850s. It was originally made with brandy, but works really well with a rye whiskey too. The rinse of absinthe adds an intricate layer of complexity to the drink.

- Stir all the ingredients, except the absinthe, in a mixing glass filled with ice. Rinse a chilled rocks glass with the absinthe. Strain the contents of the mixing glass into the rocks glass and garnish with a thin zest of lemon.

Mix It Up

Instead of using sugar syrup, muddle a brown sugar cube with a little water and the rye whiskey, before straining into the absinthe rinsed glass. A bit more time consuming, but this will add a richness to the flavour of the cocktail.

WHISKEY MAC
pictured opposite, left

50 ml/2 oz. whiskey

50 ml/2 oz. green ginger wine

a twist of lemon zest

ginger ale or ginger beer (optional)

For people who like their drinks spicy but not too sweet. For a weaker version, serve in a long glass and top up with a soft drink.

• Shake the whiskey, ginger wine and ice cubes in a cocktail shaker. Strain into a small glass and serve with a twist of lemon zest.

WHISKEY SOUR
pictured opposite, right

Probably the most popular of all sour drinks, this is one sophisticated tipple.

• Add the lemon juice, sugar syrup, bourbon whiskey and Angostura bitters to the shaker and shake. Pour into a rocks glass filled with ice. Garnish with the lemon zest.

freshly squeezed juice of 1 lemon

2½ barspoons sugar syrup (page 91)

50 ml/2 oz. bourbon whiskey

a few drops of Angostura bitters (optional)

lemon zest, to garnish

BOSTON SOUR

50 ml/2 oz. bourbon

25 ml/1 oz. fresh lemon juice

2 barspoons sugar syrup (page 91)

2 dashes of Angostura bitters

a dash of egg white

lemon slice and maraschino cherry, to garnish

A variation on the Whiskey Sour (page 72) with the addition of an egg white. Scotch or bourbon will work but bourbon brings a vanillary sweetness that is fantastic.

- Add all the ingredients to a shaker filled with ice and shake sharply. Strain the contents into a rocks glass filled with ice, garnish with a lemon slice and a maraschino cherry.

BOURBON COBBLER

For a deliciously tropical alternative to a Mint Julep (page 63), try a refreshing Bourbon Cobbler. Gently ease the juice out of the fruit for a sharp citrus flavour.

- Gently muddle the fruit in a rocks glass, add the bourbon, curaçao and ice and stir well. Add more ice and stir again, garnish with a sprig of fresh mint and serve with two short straws.

a pineapple slice
an orange slice
a lemon slice
50 ml/2 oz. bourbon
15 ml/½ oz. orange curaçao
a fresh mint sprig, to garnish

KENTUCKY

5 fresh mint leaves

15 ml/½ oz. passion fruit purée

1 passion fruit

25 ml/1 oz. apple juice

15 ml/½ oz. sugar syrup (page 91)

50 ml/2 oz. Jack Daniel's single barrel whiskey

½ passion fruit and a fresh mint sprig, to garnish

If you are mad about both whiskey and passion fruit you will adore this cocktail. The fruit and mint not only bring a delicious freshness to the drink, but also balance the warmth of the Jack Daniel's.

• Muddle the mint with the passion fruit purée in a shaker. Halve the passion fruit and scoop the pulp into the shaker, add the remaining ingredients, and top up with ice. Shake. Double-strain into a martini glass, then garnish with the passion fruit and mint.

Mix It Up

Try a pomegranate purée (strained) instead of the passion fruit purée. Garnish with a few beautiful pomegranate seeds.

LYNCHBURG LEMONADE

2 lemon wedges

2 barspoons caster/
granulated sugar

50 ml/2 oz. Jack Daniel's

lemonade, to top up

You may see variations of this recipe using triple sec or Cointreau as the sweetening agent. This version uses sugar for its coarseness and fresh lemon wedges muddled together for a more 'rustic' feel.

• Muddle the lemon and sugar together in a highball glass. Add ice and the remaining ingredients. Stir gently and serve with two straws.

Mix It Up

Replace the caster/granulated sugar with 2 barspoons of grenadine syrup to make a Pink Lynchburg Lemonade that is pretty as a picture. Garnish with fresh mint leaves for that extra flourish.

HOT TODDY

50 ml/2 oz. Scotch whisky

20 ml/⅔ dark honey

25 ml/1 oz. fresh lemon juice

a pinch of ground cinnamon or 1 cinnamon stick

boiling water, to top up

2 pieces of lemon zest, studded with cloves, to garnish

For some reason this drink is often only consumed when the drinker feels under the weather, but the hot toddy is some people's winter warmer of choice. It's perfect for sipping after any outdoor activity when things have turned frosty.

- Add all the ingredients to a heatproof glass or pewter tankard and stir gently to mix. Top up with boiling water and serve garnished with a piece of lemon zest studded with cloves.

Mix It Up

A Hot Ginger Toddy is a wonderful variation to try because ginger is the perfect complement to whiskey. Just add 15 ml/ ½ oz. ginger liqueur in place of the cinnamon and cloves.

BLUE BLAZER *pictured opposite*

1 sugar cube
50 ml/2 oz. boiling water
50 ml/2 oz. whiskey
grated nutmeg, to garnish

A spectacular drink, but one that is best practised in the safe confines of the kitchen before trying it in front of an audience.

- Warm two small metal tankards. In one, dissolve the sugar in the boiling water. Pour the whiskey into the other. Set the whiskey alight and, as it burns, pour the liquid into the first tumbler and back, from one to another, creating a continuous stream of fire. Once the flame has died down, pour the mixture into a warmed old-fashioned glass and garnish with a sprinkling of grated nutmeg.

RUSTY NAIL

This one's purely for the colder months, when you are curled up in front of an open fire with a good book.

30 ml/1¼ oz. whiskey
30 ml/1¼ oz. Drambuie
orange zest, to garnish

- Add both ingredients to a glass filled with ice and muddle with a barspoon. Garnish with orange zest.

SALTED CARAMEL BOURBON MILKSHAKE

1 litre/4 cups salted caramel ice cream

250 ml/1 cup chocolate milk

1 teaspoon sea salt

150 ml/⅔ cup bourbon

This adults–only milkshake combines the best of both worlds — milkshake and bourbon. This recipe serves 4 people, it is simply too good to keep to yourself.

• Blend the ice cream, chocolate milk, sea salt and bourbon in a blender, adding ice depending how thick you want your shake. Pour into lowball glasses or tumblers.

Mix It Up

Try using good quality chocolate ice cream instead of salted caramel for an intensely chocolatey hit. Add a sprinkle of grated chocolate or a topping of whipped cream and caramel sauce for even more indulgence.

RUM

MOJITO
pictured opposite

2 lime wedges

2 barspoons caster/
granulated sugar

9 fresh mint sprigs

50 ml/2 oz. light rum

a dash of soda water

sugar syrup, to taste (page 91)

The Mojito has had a big revival on the cocktail scene. Here is the classic recipe.

- Muddle the lime, sugar and mint (reserving 1 sprig for the garnish) in the bottom of a highball glass, fill with plenty of crushed ice and add the rum. Stir well and add a dash of soda water. Add a dash or two of sugar syrup, to taste. Garnish with the mint sprig and serve.

RASPBERRY & ROSE MOJITO

This raspberry—and—rose Mojito makes for a delicate and enchanting cocktail.

- Pour the rose syrup into a highball glass. Add the mint leaves and rum. Delicately press the mint with the back of a barspoon. Add the lime juice and enough ice to come two-thirds of the way up the glass. Gently churn with the spoon. Pile up with more crushed ice and drizzle over the crème de framboise. Garnish with rose petals and mint.

15 ml/½ oz. rose syrup

8 fresh mint leaves

50 ml/2 oz. light rum

freshly squeezed juice of 1 lime

15 ml/½ oz. crème de framboise

2 rose petals and a fresh mint
sprig, to garnish

ORIGINAL DAIQUIRI

50 ml/2 oz. golden rum

20 ml/⅔ oz. fresh lime juice

2 barspoons sugar syrup
(page 91)

This classic cocktail was made famous at the El Floridita restaurant, Havana, early in the 20th century. Experiment to find your perfect balance of golden rum, sharp citrus juice and sweet sugar syrup.

- Pour all the ingredients into an ice-filled shaker. Shake and strain into a chilled martini glass.

ORANGE DAIQUIRI *pictured opposite*

The Orange Daiquiri substitutes the sweet Martinique rum called Creole Shrub for the Cuban rum of the Original Daiquiri, so uses a little less sugar syrup.

- Pour all the ingredients into an ice-filled shaker. Shake and strain into a chilled martini glass.

50 ml/2 oz. Creole Shrub rum

20 ml/⅔ oz. fresh lime juice

1 barspoon sugar syrup
(page 91)

THE LOUNGER

25 ml/1 oz. fresh lime juice

25 ml/1 oz. vanilla-infused rum

25 ml/1 oz. ginger cordial

¼ teaspoon sugar syrup (see method)

1 glacé/candied cherry, to garnish

The title of this cocktail incorporates the names of the ingredients, rather than referring to your likely activities after you've drunk a few, by the way. It will work nicely with light or dark rum.

- To make the sugar syrup, put 2 parts caster/granulated sugar to 1 part water in a saucepan (the quantities depend, of course, on how much you want to make), and boil until the sugar has just dissolved. Leave to cool completely before using.

- Measure the lime, rum, ginger and sugar syrup into a cocktail shaker. Add a couple of ice cubes, replace the lid and shake hard. Pour into a cocktail glass and add a glacé/candied cherry if you want a touch of extra sweetness.

Mix It Up

Golden rum can be infused with all manner of delicious delicacies. Make your own spiced rum by popping a cinnamon stick, cloves, star anise and orange zest into a bottle of golden rum and leaving to impart flavour for at least 24 hours.

BACARDI COCKTAIL

50 ml/2 oz. Bacardi white rum
3 barspoons grenadine
20 ml/⅔ oz. fresh lime juice

One of the best-known Daiquiri variations and one that must be made with the Bacardi brand of white rum, as decreed by a New York court action in 1936.

- Shake all the ingredients sharply over ice, then strain into a chilled martini glass and serve.

Mix It Up

Try making a Sour Bacardi Cocktail by replacing the grenadine with a sour mix syrup and the lime juice with apple juice. The luminous green colour will be quite the opposite of the pink drink pictured.

HURRICANE
pictured opposite

50 ml/2 oz. dark rum
25 ml/1 oz. fresh lemon juice
25 ml/1 oz. passion fruit syrup
passion fruit juice (optional)
passion fruit seeds, to garnish

This cocktail was created by Pat O'Brien in his New Orleans tavern in the 1940s. Try to use proper passion fruit syrup instead of ready-made hurricane mix.

- Add all the ingredients to a cocktail shaker filled with ice and shake vigorously to mix.
- Strain into a hurricane glass or tiki mug filled with crushed ice, top up with passion fruit juice, if using, and serve garnished with passion fruit seeds.

BAY BREEZE

An uncomplicated and refreshing cocktail, but don't be fooled into thinking this one tastes better with vodka.

50 ml/2 oz. golden rum
100 ml/4 oz. cranberry juice
50 ml/2 oz. pineapple juice
lime wedge, to garnish

- Add all the ingredients to a shaker filled with ice, shake and strain into a highball glass filled with ice. Garnish with a lime wedge.

GINGER RUM

1 piece stem ginger, crushed
to a purée

1 barspoon ginger syrup
from the jar

60 ml/2¼ oz. golden rum

15 ml/½ oz. fresh lime juice

lime wedge, to garnish

Rum and ginger make a marriage made in heaven — the very essence of the tropics! Golden rum from Barbados is a wonderful compromise between the elegance of white rum and the power–flavour of dark rum. The result is a delightful golden colour. Serve as a cocktail, or as a long drink with your favourite mixer.

- Crush the stem ginger to a purée with a fork, and scrape into a shaker. Add the ginger syrup, rum, lime juice and ice.

- Shake well, then strain into a glass filled with ice and garnish with a wedge of lime. Add extra syrup if you prefer a sweeter drink. Alternatively, whizz in a blender, then strain over ice.

- For a long drink, serve in a Collins glass topped with ginger ale or soda.

CUBA LIBRE

One of the most famous of all rum–based drinks was reputed to have been invented by an army officer in Cuba shortly after Coca Cola was first produced in the 1890s.

50 ml/2 oz. white rum
1 lime
cola, to top up

- Pour the rum into a highball filled with ice; cut a lime into eighths, squeeze and drop the wedges into the glass. Top with cola and serve with straws.

PIÑA COLADA

50 ml/2 oz. golden rum
25 ml/1 oz. coconut cream
15 ml/½ oz. single/light cream
25 ml/1 oz. pineapple juice

A sweet, creamy drink that, for a time, epitomized the kind of cocktail that 'real' cocktail drinkers disapproved of (compare the somewhat ostentatious Piña Colada with a simple Dry Martini!). However, since its creation in the 1970s, it has won widespread popularity, and now that we are in the new millennium, cocktails are for everyone so there's no shame in ordering a Piña Colada at the bar.

• Put all the ingredients into a blender, add a scoop of crushed ice and blend. Pour into a sour or collins glass and garnish with a thick slice of pineapple.

Mix It Up

Be warned, this variation is only for the very sweet toothed! For a Honey Colada, add 2 barspoons of honey or sugar syrup to the glass after the drink has been poured. A sweet surprise will be left lurking at the bottom of the glass.

MON CHERI

pictured opposite, right*

50 ml/2 oz. Grand Marnier

25 ml/1 oz. rum

2 tablespoons finely grated dark/bittersweet chocolate

15 ml/½ oz. cherry liqueur

2 barspoons cider vinegar

Vinegar–based cocktails are a fashionable favourite on the London cocktail circuit and rightly so. The vinegar cuts through the sweetness of the cocktail, adding a delicious sweet and sour flavour. You may have difficulty stopping at one glass! This one is for all those chocolate and cherry lovers out there.

• Shake all the ingredients together and serve with ice.

Mix It Up

If you fancy this cocktail without the sour edge of the cider vinegar, replace it with 2 barspoons of chocolate liqueur. It will taste like black forest gâteau in a glass.

*pictured opposite, left. Queen of Tarts—see page 27 for recipe

DARK & STORMY

pictured opposite

60 ml/2¼ oz. Goslings Black Seal rum or similar

ginger beer, to top up

lime wedges, to serve

Dark & Stormy is hailed as the national drink of Bermuda. Although its name sounds like trouble it is refreshing served over ice. Homemade ginger beer gives this drink a zestier flavour.

• Fill a chilled glass with crushed ice. Pour in the rum and top with ginger beer. Finish with a squeeze of lime and serve.

DARK & STRAWMY

Adding fresh strawberries to this cocktail lightens some of the heavier rum flavours and makes the drink a little sweeter.

3 lime slices

2 strawberries, sliced, plus extra to garnish

50 ml/2 oz. dark rum

ginger beer, to top up

• Muddle the lime and the strawberries in a highball glass. Add ice and the remaining ingredients and stir gently. Serve with a straw and half a strawberry to garnish.

BALTIMORE EGGNOG

25 ml/1 oz. Madeira wine
15 ml/½ oz. Cognac
15 ml/½ oz. Jamaican rum
a pinch of ground cinnamon
1 tablespoon caster/
granulated sugar
1 egg
25 ml/1 oz. double/heavy cream
grated nutmeg, to serve

In essence, eggnog is a mixture of cream (or milk), sugar and beaten egg that can have alcohol added to it. Of the many variations around, Baltimore Eggnog is possibly the best: three different types of liquor as well as the dusting of spice really add extra depth.

- Add all the ingredients to a cocktail shaker and shake vigorously for 15 seconds.
  - Pour into a glass and grate over a little nutmeg, to serve.

HOT BUTTERED RUM

Rum may be the perfect ingredient for a summer Caribbean–style cocktail, but it also happily lends itself to those winter nights, with the sweetness of the rum combining with the spices and the brown sugar. Try also adding cinnamon or vanilla to the mix for added complexity.

3 teaspoons brown sugar

50 ml/2 oz. dark rum

½ teaspoon allspice

1 teaspoon butter

hot water, to top up

orange zest studded with cloves, to garnish

- Warm a heat-resistant glass and add the sugar and a little hot water. Stir until the sugar has dissolved and then add the rum, allspice and butter. Top up with hot water and stir until the butter has melted.

- Garnish with a piece of orange zest studded with cloves, and serve.

TEQUILA

CLASSIC MARGARITA

pictured opposite

50 ml/2 oz. gold tequila

25 ml/1 oz. triple sec or Cointreau

freshly squeezed juice of ½ lime

salt, for the glass

Treat this cool cocktail with the respect it deserves. Stay away from premixes, too much ice and cordial. Instead use fresh lemon or lime and gold tequila, which usually has a smoother taste than silver.

- Shake all the ingredients sharply with crushed ice then strain into a frosted margarita glass rimmed with salt.

LAHARA MARGARITA

Named after the oranges grown on the island of Curaçao, the Lahara fruit is inedibly bitter — it is the zest that is used to flavour the blue curaçao.

- Add all the ingredients to a shaker filled with crushed ice. Shake and then strain into a frosted margarita glass or punch cup.

50 ml/2 oz. reposado tequila

20 ml/⅔ oz. blue curaçao

20 ml/⅔ oz. triple sec

freshly squeezed juice of ½ lime

FROZEN PEACH MARGARITA

¼ teaspoon chipotle chilli/
chili powder

1 tablespoon sea salt flakes

50 ml/2 oz. tequila

25 ml/1 oz. peach schnapps

1 fresh peach, pitted and
quartered, or 225 g/½ lb.
frozen peaches

finely grated zest and freshly
squeezed juice of 1 lime

The Frozen Peach Margarita is a real crowd pleaser on a warm day. It is best made in season when peaches are ripe and juicy, but you can also use frozen peaches. The chilli/chili salt adds a taste of Mexico.

• Mix together the chilli/chili powder and salt flakes. Wet the rim of a glass with the squeezed lime and dip into the chilli/chili salt. Set aside.

• Put the remaining ingredients in a blender and blend until smooth. Serve in the salted glass.

Mix It Up

When it comes to frozen Margaritas, the world of fruit is your oyster! Blood orange, pear, strawberry, kiwi, pineapple; any fruit with soft and tender flesh will work. Don't forget to replace the peach schnapps with the corresponding flavour. You could also try a Frozen Coconut Margarita variation using coconut cream for a gorgeous rich and creamy finish.

MANGORITA

pictured opposite

50 ml/2 oz. gold tequila
20 ml/⅔ oz. triple sec
20 ml/⅔ oz. fresh lime juice
25 ml/1 oz. mango purée
(or ¼ peeled mango)
mango slice, to garnish

This cocktail is an easy one to make, but very tricky to get right: mango is a powerfully flavoured fruit but you still need to be able to taste the tequila.

• Add all the ingredients to a blender. Add two scoops of crushed ice and blend for 20 seconds. Pour into a margarita coupette and garnish with a slice of mango.

PIÑARITA

The combination of pineapple and tequila results in a truly tropical flavour. This one deserves to be decorated lavishly.

• Add all the ingredients to a blender. Add two scoops of crushed ice and blend for 20 seconds. Pour into a hurricane glass, garnish with a pineapple slice and serve with a couple of straws.

50 ml/2 oz. gold tequila
20 ml/⅔ oz. triple sec
20 ml/⅔ oz. fresh lime juice
25 ml/1 oz. pineapple juice
pineapple slice, to garnish

LAGERITA

1 lime

25 ml/1 oz. gold tequila

1 brown sugar cube

Negra Modello, or other dark beer, to top up

This is a tequila–based drink for the more adventurous among us. It is essential that a dark beer is used.

- Cut the lime into quarters, squeeze and drop them into a highball glass. Add the tequila and the sugar cube and muddle using a barspoon. Fill the glass with ice and add the dark beer.

- Muddle again, ensuring as much of the sugar as possible has dissolved. Serve with two straws.

Mix It Up

Not a beer drinker? Try a Ciderita. Cider will be sweet enough to hold its own in this cocktail, so omit the sugar cube and combine the tequila and lime with a cider of your choice, muddling together as in the recipe above. Garnish the glass with apple slices.

SALTY CHIHUAHUA *pictured opposite*

50 ml/2 oz. gold tequila
200 ml/8 oz. grapefruit juice
lime wedge, to garnish
salt, for the rim

A variation on the classic Salty Dog, which uses gin or vodka, this cocktail is a recommended morning–after fix. A simple combination that can cut through the fog of any hangover.

- Pour the tequila into a salt-rimmed highball glass filled with ice. Top with grapefruit juice, garnish with a lime wedge and serve with two straws.

SWEET CHIHUAHUA

A sweet and refreshing variation of the recipe above. The sugar on the rim of the glass is delicious with the sour grapefruit.

- Pour the tequila and hibiscus cordial into a sugar-edged highball glass filled with ice. Top with the grapefruit juice, garnish with a lime wedge and serve.

50 ml/2 oz. tequila
a dash of hibiscus cordial
200 ml/8 oz. grapefruit juice
lime wedge, to garnish
sugar, for the rim

DIABLO

50 ml/2 oz. gold tequila
15 ml/½ oz. fresh lime juice
15 ml/½ oz. crème de cassis
ginger ale, to top up
redcurrants, to garnish

The Diablo is a long and refreshing classic cocktail that dates back to the 1940s. The spice of the ginger is soothed by the delicate hint of blackcurrant and invigorated by the fresh lime.

• Build all the ingredients in a hurricane glass filled with crushed ice. Garnish with a small bunch of redcurrants and a devil fork swizzle stick.

TRES COMPADRES

The combination of lime, orange and grapefruit juice provide the three citrus compadres. Cointreau and Chambord are then added to the mix to sweeten, and lo and behold a great cocktail is born. Try serving this long (by adding more orange and grapefruit juice) for an extra-refreshing cooler.

50 ml/2 oz. gold tequila
20 ml/⅔ oz. Cointreau
20 ml/⅔ oz. Chambord
25 ml/1 oz. fresh lime juice
20 ml/⅔ oz. orange juice
20 ml/⅔ oz. grapefruit juice
lime wedge, to garnish
salt, for the glass

• Add all the ingredients to a shaker filled with ice. Shake sharply and strain into a chilled margarita glass edged with salt. Garnish with a lime wedge.

GREEN IGUANA *pictured opposite*

50 ml/2 oz. Sauza Hornitos
tequila

25 ml/1 oz. Midori

25 ml/1 oz. fresh lime juice

The combination of melon and tequila works perfectly here. Midori (a melon-flavoured liqueur) is used in this recipe as fresh melon is not quite sweet enough.

- Add all the ingredients to a shaker filled with ice. Shake sharply and strain into a rocks glass filled with ice.

HORNY TOAD

Made using Sauza Hornitos tequila, the Horny Toad is named after the creature used to exemplify ugliness in Mexico. Strangely enough, you may find everyone much more attractive after drinking this!

- Add all the ingredients to a shaker filled with ice. Shake sharply and strain into an ice-filled margarita glass, rimmed with salt.

35 ml/1¼ oz. Sauza Hornitos
tequila

25 ml/1 oz. Cointreau

40 ml/1½ oz. fresh lime or
lemon juice

salt, for the glass

PALOMA PUNCH

500 ml/2 cups reposado tequila

100 ml/⅓ cup agave syrup

1.5 litres/6 cups grapefruit juice

3 limes

soda water, to top up

salt, for the glass

The literal meaning of paloma is 'dove', although why this drink is so called is a mystery! Although it may seem a lot of effort, do try, where possible, to use freshly squeezed grapefruit juice for this cocktail. This recipe will make enough punch to serve 10 people. Party time!

- Put the tequila, agave syrup, and grapefruit juice in a jug/pitcher filled with ice. Squeeze the limes into the pitcher and drop the husks in too, reserving one for preparing the glasses. Top up with the soda water and stir gently to mix.

- To prepare the glasses, pour some salt onto a plate. Rub the rim of the glasses with the spent lime husk. Turn each glass upside down and place it in the salt so that it coats the rim.

- Fill the salt-rimmed glasses with ice, top up with punch and serve.

RED CACTUS

The fresh raspberries and Chambord in this drink team up to provide a fruity punch that almost masks the flavour of its base spirit. Don't be deceived; there's still plenty of tequila in here.

- Add all the ingredients to a blender. Add two scoops of crushed ice and blend for 20 seconds.
- Pour into a margarita coupette or hurricane glass. Garnish with lime slices and serve immediately.

50 ml/2 oz. Sauza Extra Gold tequila

20 ml/⅔ oz. triple sec

20 ml/⅔ oz. Chambord

35 ml/1¼ oz. fresh lime juice

4 fresh raspberries

lime slices, to garnish

SILK STOCKING

35 ml/1¼ oz. gold tequila

15 ml/½ oz. white crème de cacao

15 ml/½ oz. grenadine

15 ml/½ oz. double/heavy cream

2 fresh raspberries, to garnish

This tequila drink was invented during the 1920s in the US, at a time when cocktails were often given names revelling in innuendo and sensuality.

- Add all the ingredients to a blender. Add two scoops of crushed ice and blend for 20 seconds. Pour the mixture into a hurricane glass, garnish with two raspberries and serve with two straws.

Mix It Up

Take away the grenadine and you are left with a snowy white 'Frostbite' cocktail. Alternatively, add a delicate dash of blue curaçao instead of the grenadine and you will be left with a baby blue 'Satin Stocking'.

BRANDY, LIQUEURS & APERITIFS

HORSE'S NECK

50 ml/2 oz. VSOP Cognac
10 drops of Angostura bitters
ginger ale, to top up
lemon twist, to garnish

When you are dealing with strong flavours, such as bitters, you have to be cautious about the amount of drops or dashes you use in a cocktail. It's all a question of getting the balance right. Here, the Horse's Neck, which has been highly popular ever since the 1930s, is a finely balanced example of a classic cocktail that first appeared, in the States, over a century ago.

• Prepare a tall glass with the garnish of a large lemon twist. Fill with ice cubes and add the ingredients; then stir.

Mix It Up

Replacing the traditional large lemon twist garnish with a twist of orange zest will add a subtle difference in flavour to this old-timer.

SIDECAR

50 ml/2 oz. brandy
20 ml/⅔ oz. fresh lemon juice
20 ml/⅔ oz. Cointreau
sugar, for the glass

The Sidecar, like many of the classic cocktails created in the 1920s, is attributed to the inventive genius of Harry McElhone, who founded Harry's New York Bar in Paris. It is said to have been created in honour of an eccentric military man who would roll up outside the bar in the sidecar of his chauffeur–driven motorcycle.

- Shake all the ingredients together over ice and strain into a chilled martini glass with a sugared edge.

Mix It Up

Try a subtle switch to prevent messing with this classic too much: replace the regular brandy with calvados to create a sophisticated Apple Sidecar.

APRICOT ROYALE

pictured opposite

50 ml/2 oz. apricot brandy
20 ml/⅔ oz. fresh lemon juice
20 ml/⅔ oz. sugar syrup
(page 91)
a dash of peach bitters
a dash of orange bitters
champagne, to float
apricot slice, to garnish

Serve this one to guests who need a bit of livening up! The fruity melody of flavours combines with the champagne to make this drink the perfect cure for the blues.

- Add all the ingredients, except the champagne, to a shaker filled with ice, shake sharply and strain into a rocks glass filled with ice. Gently layer a float of champagne over the surface of the drink. Garnish with an apricot slice and serve.

BLOOD & SAND

This cocktail is an example of how a drink should never be judged by anything less than the sum of its parts. It should taste like your favourite festive pudding.

25 ml/1 oz. Scotch whisky
25 ml/1 oz. sweet vermouth
25 ml/1 oz. cherry brandy
25 ml/1 oz. orange juice

- Add all the ingredients to a shaker filled with ice, shake sharply then strain into a frosted martini glass.

PISCO SOUR

50 ml/2 oz. pisco
25 ml/1 oz. fresh lemon juice
15 ml/½ oz. sugar syrup
(page 91)
15 ml/½ oz. egg white
2 dashes of Angostura bitters

Pisco is a type of brandy produced in Peru and Chile, it is so popular in its native Peru that there is actually a 'national pisco day'. This cocktail is a shining example of how a cocktail can bring to light an underappreciated spirit.

• Add all the ingredients to a shaker filled with ice. Shake sharply and strain into a champagne flute.

SOUR ITALIAN

25 ml/1 oz. Campari

15 ml/½ oz. Strega

15 ml/½ oz. Galliano

25 ml/1 oz. fresh lemon juice

15 ml/½ oz. cranberry juice

15 ml/½ oz. sugar syrup (page 91)

a dash of egg white

2 dashes of Angostura bitters

A cocktail made completely from Italian ingredients, the Sour Italian makes a lovely aperitif.

• Shake all the ingredients over ice and strain into a chilled champagne flute.

BLUEBERRY AMARETTO SOUR

pictured opposite

50 ml/2 oz. blueberry-infused amaretto*

25 ml/1 oz. fresh lemon juice

If you want to add that special touch to a cocktail and don't mind putting in a bit of work, then this is well worth the effort.

- Add all the ingredients to a shaker filled with ice, shake sharply and strain into a pre-chilled liqueur glass.

*Blueberry-infused amaretto: Pierce ten blueberries with a knife and place them in a bottle of Amaretto. Leave them to infuse for a few days, shaking occasionally, and taste. Pass the mixture through a fine strainer before using it.

MIDORI SOUR

Shake this one hard, go gentle on the sugar syrup and you'll have a great–tasting, balanced and dramatic–looking cocktail.

- Add all the ingredients to a shaker filled with ice, shake sharply and strain into a rocks glass filled with ice. Garnish with a lemon wheel and serve with two short straws.

50 ml/2 oz. Midori

25 ml/1 oz. fresh lemon juice

1 barspoon sugar syrup (page 91)

a dash of egg white

lemon wheel, to garnish

CAIPIRINHA

1 lime

2 brown sugar cubes

50 ml/2 oz. cachaça

sugar syrup, to taste
(page 91)

Cachaça, a spirit indigenous to Brazil, is distilled directly from the juice of sugar cane. The Caipirinha has made cachaça popular in many countries.

- Cut the lime into eighths, squeeze and place in an old-fashioned glass with the sugar cubes, then pound well with a pestle.
- Fill the glass with crushed ice and add the cachaça. Stir vigorously and add sugar syrup, to taste. Serve with two straws.

Mix It Up

Cachaça actually makes a great base for a Bloody Mary in place of vodka, it adds a bit of bite to the classic hangover cure. Make a Bloody Caipirinha by referring to the rest of the ingredients and method on page 36.

GRASSHOPPER
pictured opposite, left

25 ml/1 oz. crème de menthe (white)

15 ml/½ oz. crème de menthe

25 ml/1 oz. single/light cream

A combination of peppermint and cream, the Grasshopper is the perfect drink to accompany your after–dinner coffee.

- Shake all the ingredients over ice, strain into a frosted martini glass and serve.

GOLDEN CADILLAC
pictured opposite, right

You could be excused for raising your eyebrows at the mixture of crème de cacao with orange juice and Galliano (herb and liquorice flavoured). If this is too complicated for you, try substituting the crème de cacao with Cointreau.

25 ml/1 oz. crème de cacao (white)

25 ml/1 oz. single/light cream

50 ml/2 oz. orange juice

a dash of Galliano

- Shake all the ingredients over ice, strain into a martini glass and serve.

GREEN LADY

1 egg white

40 ml/1½ oz. Calvados

15 ml/½ oz. yuzu juice

20ml/⅔ oz. sugar syrup
(page 91)

1 barspoon absinthe

1 barspoon matcha
green-tea powder

a dash of apple juice

apple slice with a drop of
bitters on it, to garnish

The Asian slant in this recipe comes from the juice of the yuzu, a citrus fruit grown in Japan, which has a distinctive flavour described by some people as a cross between mandarin and grapefruit, though others think it's more like a synthesis of lime and grapefruit. A subtle difference! See what you think when you try it.

- Put the egg white in a shaker and stir to break it down. (The egg white gives a lovely, rounded, silky texture to the cocktail.) Add the rest of the ingredients and ice. Shake, then strain into a glass.

- Garnish with the slice of apple.

Mix It Up

Bottled yuzu juice can be found at speciality food stores and Asian markets. If you can't get your hands on the yuzu juice for this recipe, replace with a mixture of 1 part grapefruit to 3 parts lime juice to create a similar flavour. Alternatively, simply use more apple juice for a sweeter finish.

ORANGE BRÛLÉE *pictured opposite*

25 ml/1 oz. Grand Marnier

15 ml/½ oz. amaretto

a dash of white crème de cacao

whipping cream, to top

orange zest, to garnish

The Orange Brûlée is a dessert drink that should be savoured. The only part missing is the blowtorch finish.

- Add all the ingredients, except the cream, to a shaker filled with ice, shake sharply then strain into a martini glass. Whip the cream and dollop gently over the surface of the drink. Criss-cross with thin strips of orange zest.

LEMON MERINGUE

Mixing citrus fruits with cream liqueurs generally isn't recommended for cocktails, but somehow this concoction resists the temptation to curdle. It is simply delicious!

- Add all the ingredients to a shaker filled with ice, shake sharply then strain into a frosted martini glass.

50 ml/2 oz. Cytryonowka vodka

20 ml/⅔ oz. lemon juice

15 ml/½ oz. Drambuie Cream

a dash of sugar syrup (page 91)

BRANDY ALEXANDER

pictured opposite

50 ml/2 oz. brandy

15 ml/½ oz. crème de cacao (dark or white)

15 ml/½ oz. double/ heavy cream

The perfect after-dinner cocktail, luscious and seductive and great for chocolate lovers. It's important, though, to get the proportions right so that the brandy stands out as the major investor.

• Shake all the ingredients over ice and strain into a frosted martini glass. Garnish with a sprinkle of nutmeg.

STINGER

A great palate cleanser and digestif which, like brandy, should be consumed after dinner. The amount of crème de menthe used depends on personal taste.

50 ml/2 oz. brandy

25 ml/1 oz. white crème de menthe

• Shake the ingredients together over ice and strain into a frosted martini glass.

LEMON DROP

50 ml/2 oz. lemon vodka
15 ml/½ oz. Cointreau
20 ml/⅔ oz. fresh lemon juice
lemon slice, to garnish

There are various ways to present this sharp shooter. You can coat a lemon slice in sugar and lay it over the surface of the glass to bite into after the shot, or you can take it one step further and soak the lemon slice in Cointreau before coating it, then set it alight!

- Add all the ingredients to a shaker filled with ice. Shake very hard and strain into a shot glass. Garnish with a lemon slice.

Mix It Up

Adding half a teaspoon of lemon sherbet powder to the shaker will really give this drink an extra sparkle. Don't add too much or the consistency will be too foamy to drink in shot form. Alternatively, lace the rim of the shot glass with the sherbet.

PURPLE HAZE

1 white sugar cube
½ lime
50 ml/2 oz. vodka
a dash of Grand Marnier
25 ml/1 oz. Chambord

The Purple Haze is a classic Kamikaze with a twist — a drink that belies its strength and will kick-start any evening's fun. Let the good times roll!

- Put a sugar cube and the fresh lime half, cut into quarters, into a shaker and crush them together with a muddler or barspoon. Add the vodka and Grand Marnier.

- Fill the shaker with ice, then shake and strain the mixture into a chilled shot glass. Float a single measure of Chambord on to the drink and serve.

Mix It Up

Take things back to basics by using just 50 ml/2 oz. vodka, 25 ml/1 oz. triple sec and the juice of half a lime to make a classic Kamikaze shooter.

B52

15 ml/½ oz. Kahlúa
15 ml/½ oz. Baileys
15 ml/½ oz. Grand Marnier

The B52 has reached the lofty peak of being regarded a classic within the world of layered drinks. This shot is best drunk after dinner, as it has a tendency to take the palate by storm.

- Layer each ingredient on top of each other over a barspoon in a shot glass.

Mix It Up

You are spoilt for choice with the variations that can be had with a B52. For a B51 replace the Grand Marnier with Frangelico, for a B53 replace with vodka and for a B54 replace with tequila. Keep going until you have exhausted all the spirits!

PIMM'S CUP

50 ml/2 oz. Pimm's No 1

250 ml/1 cup lemonade/
lemon soda

75 ml/3 oz. ginger beer

cucumber slice

lemon slice

orange slice

fresh strawberry

fresh mint sprig

The perfect summer cooler, this cocktail benefits from the addition of elaborate fruit salad type garnishes. Surprisingly, the tastiest addition to this drink is the cucumber, but strawberries are also an absolute winner. One fruit addition that doesn't really work is lime, the strong citrus juice is too overwhelming.

- Build all the ingredients in a highball glass filled with ice. Stir gently and serve with two straws.

Mix It Up

For a festive variation try making the Pimm's Winter Cup with the brandy based Pimm's No 3, apple juice and sliced apples and oranges to garnish.

also pictured: Horse's Neck (see page 125 for recipe)

CHAMPAGNE
& WINE

BELLINI *pictured opposite*

½ fresh peach, blanched

15 ml/½ oz. crème de pêche

a dash of peach bitters (optional)

champagne, to top up

peach ball, to garnish

The stylish Bellini originated in Harry's Bar in Venice in the early 1940s.

- Purée the peach in a blender and add to a champagne flute. Pour in the crème de pêche and the peach bitters, and gently top up with champagne, stirring carefully and continuously. Garnish with a peach ball in the bottom of the glass, then serve.

AL FRESCO BELLINI

A quick stir and the colourful stripes in this drink meld into a gentle, magical hue.

- To create the three layers, gently pour into the glass each ingredient in turn over the flatter end of a long, double-ended barspoon: the peach purée first, then the Apérol, followed by the champagne. Garnish with the Chinese gooseberry and rose petal. When the cocktail is ready to serve, and is in front of the drinker, stir.

20 ml/⅔ oz. peach purée

15 ml/½ oz. Apérol liqueur

champagne, chilled, to top up

Chinese gooseberry and a rose petal, to garnish

KIR ROYALE

a dash of crème de cassis

champagne, to top up

After a shaky start, the Kir Royale is now the epitome of chic sophistication. It started life as the Kir, which contained acidic white wine instead of champagne, and was labelled rinse cochon (French for 'pig rinse'). Luckily, the wine became less sharp and the drink adopted a more appropriate mantle.

- Add a small dash of crème de cassis to a champagne flute and gently top with champagne. Stir gently and serve.

Mix It Up

For an original Kir use a good quality white wine instead of champagne. A more unusual variation is a Kir Pamplemousse, made with red grapefruit liqueur as the base and topped up with sparkling white wine.

ROSSINI *pictured opposite*

15 ml/½ oz. raspberry purée

1 barspoon Chambord (optional)

2 dashes of orange bitters

champagne, to top up

A great variation on the Bellini, the Rossini can be spiced up with a little Chambord and a dash of orange bitters — two of a bartender's favourite ingredients.

- Add the purée, Chambord (if using) and bitters to a champagne flute and top gently with champagne. Stir gently and serve.

MIMOSA

It is thought that Alfred Hitchcock invented this drink sometime in the 1940s in an old San Francisco eatery called Jack's for a group of friends suffering from hangovers.

½ glass champagne

2 barspoons Grand Marnier

fresh orange juice, to top up

- Pour the orange juice over the champagne and Grand Marnier and stir gently.

PEACH BLOSSOM SPRING

25 ml/1 oz. vodka
25 ml/1 oz. peach purée
2 barspoons crème de pêche
prosecco, to top up
2 dashes peach bitters
peach slice, to garnish

This is a slight deviation of the classic Bellini, adding a little extra kick with the vodka and peach liqueur. Perfect for serving on a summer's evening or before a dinner party to get the night's proceeding off to a sophisticated start.

- Add the vodka, peach purée and crème de pêche to a cocktail shaker filled with ice and shake to mix.
- Strain into a champagne flute and top up with prosecco. Add two dashes of peach bitters and serve garnished with a fresh peach slice.

Mix It Up

A Lychee Blossom Spring is equally as delicious and great for a tropical-themed evening. Simply use a lychee purée and Liqueur de Lychees with orange bitters. Garnish with a fresh whole lychee on a toothpick.

GINGER CHAMPAGNE

2 thin slices ginger
25 ml/1 oz. vodka
champagne, to top up

The Ginger Champagne, highly recommended to all sushi lovers, uses an addition of vodka to boost its strength. The ginger combines conspiratorially with the champagne to create a cocktail that is delicate yet different enough to appease even the most sophisticated of cocktail drinkers.

• Put the ginger in a shaker and press with a barspoon or muddler to release the flavour. Add ice and the vodka, shake and strain into a champagne flute. Top with champagne and serve.

Mix It Up

Fire up the ginger element by replacing the vodka with 1 shot of ginger liqueur. Not for the faint-hearted.

LIMONCELLO CHAMPAGNE

25 ml/1 oz. limoncello

champagne, to top up

for the limoncello (makes 1 litre/4½ cups):

12 Meyer lemons

750 ml/3¼ cups vodka

200 g/1 cup caster/ granulated sugar

350 ml/1½ cups water

a large sterilized glass jar and sterilized bottles with airtight lids

A fun, refreshing drink to kick off cocktail hour. Great to serve this at parties as it is simple and fuss-free.

- Pour a splash of limoncello in the bottom of a chilled champagne glass and top with the champagne. Serve at once.

Mix It Up

- Making your own limoncello for this cocktail is easy and rewarding. Peel the lemon, avoiding the pith. Juice the lemons into a sterile glass jar and add the peeled zest. Pour in the vodka and stir. Cover and set aside at room temperature for 2 weeks.

- Make sugar syrup: bring the sugar and water to a boil in a saucepan over a medium–high heat. Reduce the heat and simmer for 10 minutes, stirring occasionally until the sugar has dissolved. Remove from the heat and allow to cool.

- Add the syrup to the Limoncello mixture, set aside for 30 minutes. Strain the liqueur through a muslin/cheesecloth into a jug/pitcher. Decant into sterilized bottles. Store in the refrigerator or freezer for up to 12 months.

FRENCH 75 *pictured opposite, left*

20 ml/⅔ oz. gin

2 barspoons fresh lemon juice

1 barspoon sugar syrup (page 91)

champagne, to top up

lemon zest, to garnish

Named after the big artillery gun from the First World War, which rattled off rounds at a rate of 30 per minute, this is a cocktail that will certainly shake you up.

- Shake the gin, lemon juice and sugar syrup over ice and strain into a champagne flute. Top with champagne and garnish with a long strip of lemon zest.

JAMES BOND *pictured opposite, right*

The naming of this cocktail is a mystery, since the eponymous spy liked his drinks shaken not stirred, as in this cocktail. Could be because it's just incredibly suave.

1 white sugar cube

2 dashes of Angostura bitters

25 ml/1 oz. vodka

champagne, to top up

- Place the sugar cube in a champagne flute and moisten with 2 dashes of Angostura bitters. Add the vodka and top up with champagne.

ELIXIR

20 ml/⅔ oz. Kammerling's Ginseng Spirit

20 ml/⅔ oz. sugar syrup (page 91)

25 ml/1 oz. jasmine pearl tea

150 ml/5 oz. champagne

fresh violets, to garnish

Kammerling's Ginseng Spirit is made up of over 45 different botanicals, which is probably why the character of this cocktail has as an 'apothecary' nuance — hence the name Elixir.

- Combine all the ingredients in a shaker. Top up with ice. Stir very gently and very briefly – this 'freshens' and cools the champagne with the ice, whilst ensuring that it is evenly distributed.

- Strain into a champagne flute. Garnish with the violets.

Mix It Up

For a variation that is also botanically blissful, use a rose or violet flavoured vodka in place of the ginseng spirit.

BLACK VELVET

½ glass Guinness

champagne, to top up

It is doubtful if there is another drink in the world that looks more tempting and drinkable than a Black Velvet. Pour this drink gently into the glass to allow for the somewhat unpredictable nature of both the Guinness and the champagne.

- Half-fill a champagne flute with Guinness, gently top with champagne, and serve.

Mix It Up

For those of us who can't always afford champagne, cider can be used instead to make a 'Poor Man's Black Velvet'. Unlike the traditional black velvet, these two ingredients do not blend well, and you will end up with a layered drink.

SANGRIA CLASSIC

1 bottle dry red wine

150 ml/⅔ cup Grand Marnier

250 ml/1 cup orange juice

50 ml/2 oz. sugar syrup
(page 91)

3 dashes of Angostura bitters

seasonal fresh fruit,
to garnish

Everyone needs to know how to make a Sangria, the good news is that there are few rules, so long as you add red wine (Spanish Rioja is good) and some fruit. This recipe makes enough to fill a jug/pitcher.

- Add all the ingredients to a jug/pitcher filled with ice and stir gently to mix. Serve in ice-filled glasses, garnished with seasonal fruit.

- For a special occasion, add a bottle of champagne to the punch bowl to give it extra fizz.

SANGRIA BLANCO

1 bottle crisp dry white wine

100 ml/⅓ cup elderflower liqueur

100 ml/⅓ cup dry vermouth

100 ml/⅓ cup Cointreau

75 ml/3 oz. fresh lemon juice (about 2 lemons)

generous 30 ml/1 oz. sugar syrup (page 91)

2 heavy dashes of grapefruit bitters

seasonal fresh fruit, to garnish

The elderflower liqueur adds a wonderful floral note to this classic summer drink and brings out the sweetness of the season's fruits. This recipe makes enough to fill a large jug/pitcher.

• Add all the ingredients to a jug/pitcher filled with ice and stir gently to mix. Serve in ice-filled glasses, garnished with seasonal fruit.

MULLED WINE

2 bottles red wine

100 ml/⅓ cup brandy

pared zest and freshly
squeezed juice of 2
clementines

pared zest of 1 lime

pared zest of 1 lemon

200 g/1 cup caster/superfine
sugar

1 cinnamon stick

4 cloves

4 pinches of grated nutmeg

1 split vanilla pod/bean

lemon zest and cinnamon
sticks, to garnish

Traditionally made with red wine, sugar and spices, this drink is always served hot. Try not to let your mixture boil when you heat it as this may impair the flavour. This recipe makes enough to serve 10 people.

- Add all the ingredients to a large saucepan set over medium heat. Simmer gently for about 30 minutes, stirring occasionally.

- Serve in heatproof glasses garnished with extra lemon zest and cinnamon sticks.

Mix It Up

Mulled cider is just as delicious to sip on a cold winter's night. Replace the regular brandy with Calvados and add the same spices and fruit to 2 large bottles of good quality cider.

INDEX

RECIPE CREDITS

Recipes by **Ben Reed** with the
following exceptions:

Carol Hilker
Salted Caramel Bourbon Milkshake

Elsa Petersen-Schepelern
Ginger Rum
Mint Julep
Watermelon Gin
Whiskey Mac

Janet Sawyer
The Lounger
White Lady with Vanilla

Shelagh Ryan
Best Ever Bloody Mary

Ursula Ferrigno
Mon Cheri
Queen of tarts

Valerie Aikman-Smith
Dark and Stormy
Frozen Peach Margarita
Limoncello Champagne

William Yeoward
Al Fresco Bellini
Almond Vodka Espresso
Apple Martini
Caramel Rob Roy
Classic Martini
Elixir
Green Lady
Horse's Neck
Kentucky
Maple and Walnut Old Fashioned
Negroni
Raspberry and Rose Mojito
Whiskey Sour

PICTURE CREDITS

Key: a = above; b = below; r = right;
l = left; c = centre

Jan Baldwin
100

Peter Cassidy
84

Jonathan Gregson
5cr, 109

Gavin Kingcome
12, 15, 34, 47, 74, 76, 124, 139, 167

Erin Kunkel
5br, 103, 163

William Lingwood
1, 3, 5bl, 5ar, 6, 9, 11, 16, 19, 24–26,
30, 33, 38–45, 48, 55, 56, 62–70, 75,
79, 80, 83, 86, 89, 93, 94, 97, 99,
104–106, 110–114, 117–120, 122,
127, 128, 130–136, 140–160, 164,
168–172

James Merrell
59, 73, 96

Gareth Morgans
5cl, 5al, 20, 23, 29, 51, 52, 116, 121

Steve Painter
2, 60, 90

Kate Whitaker
37